Michael Tyler

PICTURES BY Mic Looby

IT'S TRUE!

FROGS ARE CANNIBALS

ALLEN&UNWIN

For Tony Peart

who asked the first question

First published in 2004

Allen & Unwin
83 Alexander Street
Crows Nest NSW 2065
Australia
Phone: (61 2) 8425 0100
Fax: (61 2) 9906 2218
Email: info@allenandunwin.com
Web: www.allenandunwin.com

National Library of Australia
Cataloguing-in-Publication entry:

Tyler, Michael J., 1937– .
It's true! Frogs are cannibals.
Bibliography.
Includes index.
ISBN 1 74114 271 7.
1. Frogs – Juvenile literature. 2. Toads – Juvenile literature.
I. Looby, Mic. II. Title.
597.8592

Series, cover and text design by Ruth Grüner
Cover photograph: Gail Shumway/Getty Images
Set in 12.5pt Minion by Ruth Grüner
Printed by McPherson's Printing Group

3 5 7 9 10 8 6 4 2

**Teaching notes for the It's True! series are available
on the website: www.itstrue.com.au**

CONTENTS

WHY FROGS?

One question at a time please people

Some people would call me a mad professor. I spend a lot of my time going on frog-finding expeditions, doing experiments with frogs, watching what they do and telling other people about them. I go on radio and TV shows to talk about frogs. Almost every day someone writes, emails or phones me with a frog question.

In this book, you'll read about frogs the size of your fingernail, and frogs big enough to dance with. You'll meet Gross Gertrude, the frog who ate her husband – yes, many frogs are cannibals. You'll hear about toad tunnels and toad-skin tobacco, frogs whose poison could kill you, and frogs that can cure illness. You'll find out how frogs breathe with their skin, swallow with their eyeballs and drink through their backsides (it's true; everything in this book is true).

Start where you like, leapfrog to whatever catches your eye, and have a good time!

Michael J. Ty

CHAPTER 1

OF SKINS AND SKELETONS

THE BARE, BONY FACTS

Frogs don't *look* bony. You'd think they were just gristle and skin, but they do have a skeleton. It's not too different from any other land animal's skeleton, with skull bones, backbones and tailbone. But some frogs have *green* bones, no one knows why.

We know from fossils that frogs have lived on this planet for 230 million years – since the time of the dinosaurs. (Humans have existed for only one million years.) The fossil frogs aren't too different from the ones we have today, so it seems that the original frogs were well designed for life on Earth.

Frogs and toads[1] belong to the group of animals we call Amphibia. This doesn't mean they go in and out of water all the time. It means they have a double life: the first part is spent in water (as tadpoles), and the second on land. Unlike their cousins, the newts and salamanders, they are tailless amphibians.

HAVING YOUR SKIN AND EATING IT TOO

Our skin rubs off in tiny pieces all the time,[2] but snakes and large lizards slip off the whole thing all at once. This is called sloughing (sluff-ing) or ecdysis.

---

[1] Almost everything I say in this book about frogs is true of toads as well. I just didn't want to keep saying frogsandtoads all the time.

[2] I read once that at least 10 per cent of the household 'dust' collected in a vacuum cleaner is dead skin.

Frogs go one step further. They slough their skin, and then eat it![3]

How does sloughing work? Glands in the skin secrete mucus (slimy stuff), and this separates the dead skin from the living skin beneath it. When the time comes, the frog frantically twists its body, and puffs up and shrinks itself over and over again, to get rid of the skin. People who see their pet frogs contorting themselves like this think they are about to die! Finally the skin splits – then the frog stuffs it in its mouth and swallows it. A frog shedding and eating its skin is not a pretty sight.

It happens often, too – a well-fed captive frog will shed its skin about once a week.

Frogs' skin is incredibly useful. It's used for breathing and drinking. Perhaps that's why they don't want to lose it.

[3] Monkeys eat bits of skin as part of their grooming process, but the frog is the only animal that recycles everything.

THREE WAYS OF DRINKING . . . AND TWO OF THEM ARE RUDE

We think of 'drinking' as taking in water (or other liquids) through the mouth. Frogs *never* drink this way. They have three main ways of taking in water.

You'd never guess it, but insects can be up to 95 per cent water. Frogs absorb water when they digest insect prey.

This one is hard to believe. Frogs drink through their backsides! They can soak up moisture through their skin; and the area of skin that does it best is the 'seat patch'. The skin on the frog's backside is grainy, or bumpy, and this gives a larger surface in contact with the moisture. If a frog becomes dehydrated (dried out), it will sit with its seat patch pressed hard against a moist surface.

Some frogs have grooves running up the inside of the thigh leading to their cloaca (like our anus).

In this way, frogs take up water when they are in a moist place, and they lose it when their surroundings are dry. In and out all the time.

Frogs have big bladders, and will often squirt out the contents when you pick them up!

THREE WAYS OF BREATHING, TOO

If you watch a frog at rest, you'll see that its 'chest' doesn't move much, but its throat goes in and out a lot. What's going on?

The frog is breathing through its lungs (taking in a gas called oxygen, sending out another gas called carbon dioxide), just as we do. But its lungs aren't very big or efficient.

It can take up oxygen much more readily through the roof of its mouth. That's why its throat goes in and out.

On the inside of our lungs are thousands of tiny branching tubes full of threadlike blood vessels, giving a huge surface that absorbs oxygen from air we breathe in. Frog lungs are just simple hollow sacs with a surface area of only a few square centimetres. They don't capture much oxygen. The roof of a frog's mouth, though, has lots of tiny blood vessels and is very good at absorbing oxygen.

There's a third way of breathing, and it's the most important. Most frog species rely mainly on their skin to take up oxygen. This works only when it's wet. This is why it's so important for frogs to have somewhere damp to stay.

Shampoo, soap, wetting agents used by gardeners and chemicals used in weed-killers are all deadly to frogs. They interfere with frogs' ability to take up oxygen through their skin.

So there are three ways for a frog to breathe: through its lungs, the inside of its mouth and its skin – especially its skin.

GO TO PAGES 65-7 FOR MORE ON THE DEADLY EFFECTS OF SHAMPOO AND WEED-KILLERS

PLEASE! WHERE ARE YOUR TABLE MANNERS?

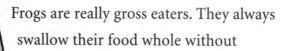

Frogs are really gross eaters. They always swallow their food whole without chewing, and they use their eyeballs – yes, their *eyeballs* – to help move food into the throat. They love to eat insects, and they really are pigs – they'll eat and eat and eat.

Frogs do have teeth, and use them to hold their prey before swallowing. They don't use teeth for chewing at all. You can understand why when you learn that they have teeth only in the upper jaw (plus sometimes an extra set in the roof of the mouth).

Most tadpoles have teeth too. Tadpole teeth are made of a black substance called keratin (the same stuff that makes fingernails and hair, horns and feathers), and there can be up to sixteen rows of them!

'KEKEKEKEKEKEKEK I LOVE YOU, BABE': FROG COURTSHIP

You've probably heard of *crooners* singing love songs – but croakers? Yes, in the world of frogs, males woo females by pretending to have laryngitis. Here's how to win the woman of your dreams in Pondland.

 Force air across your larynx (voicebox) and

 at the same time inflate the sac beneath your throat to amplify the sound. (In some species this sac looks like a pair of floaties.) If you're unlucky you won't have a sac, and your sounds will be very ˢᵒᶠᵗ. If you're lucky and you have a good big sac, you'll be very **loud** and other frogs will hear you from a kilometre away.

Each species has its own call. People who have spent a lot of time listening can recognise the different calls, just as bird-lovers can identify birds by their songs.

EAR, EAR!

Some frogs do have ears – not the outer fleshy thing that we call an ear but the bit that actually registers the sound, the eardrum. This is also called the tympanum. It's a circle of cartilage on the outside of the head just behind the eye. Sometimes the tympanum is partly or totally covered with skin. It doesn't matter – the frog can still hear perfectly well.

The interesting thing is that a frog's ears are designed to pick up calls from males of its own kind *only*. They act like a radio tuned to a particular radio station. Broadcasts from the other stations aren't 'heard' by the radio, and calls from other species are not 'heard' by a frog.

A mixed frog chorus of many species sounds like a total jumble of noise to us, but it comes across as top of the pops in Dolby™ stereo to each listening frog.

We know that frogs can also sense vibrations in the ground, because Australian Aborigines used to collect them by stamping. They said that frogs mistook the vibrations for thunder, and came out of hiding to enjoy the rain.

THE MATING URGE

When frogs are ready to mate, the males migrate to ponds and call the females in. Each female chooses the male she is most attracted to, and generally returns to the same pond each year.

Mass migrations of frogs can cause problems if there are roads on the way – problems for the frogs, that is. They get squashed in their thousands.

GO TO PAGES 24–5 FOR TOAD TUNNELS

CHAPTER 2

TADPOLES AND JELLY RAFTS

WHAT COLOUR ARE FROGS' EGGS?

When you collect frog spawn from a pond, you'll notice that the eggs are black, inside the clear jelly. Why are they not white or coloured? Ask Mum or Dad that question, and they'll say, 'Because'. When they do, you can say, 'Well, I know the answer.'

The black colour protects the eggs from harmful ultra-violet rays. Ultra-violet (UV) rays from the sun interfere with normal growth, causing abnormalities, cancers or death.

Species that lay their eggs under rocks or in other places away from the sun don't need UV protection. Their eggs are creamy white.

Now, here's a riddle. Where would you find green eggs? Up a tree, did you say? Yes, absolutely right! It sounds impossible but it's true.

The Rainbow Frog of New Guinea lays its eggs on leaves above fast-flowing creeks. Being green, they are hard to see, so they are less likely to be eaten by birds. The tadpoles don't hatch until they can swim well (they wriggle around in the jelly to practise), and then they drop into the water.

Maybe Dr Seuss knew something when he wrote *Green Eggs and Ham.*

JELLY RAFTS AND JELLY SNAKES

Lots of people have seen frog spawn in ponds or dams – a sloppy mass that collapses when you gently lift it out. Some species of frogs make jelly rafts. The female traps air bubbles with her hands and throws them into the jelly that comes out of her behind. There's even a thickshake version; groups of tree frogs beat the jelly with their legs to produce an extra-frothy mass on the leaves.

Where does the jelly come from, and what's it for?

The jelly is made inside the female frog's body. Her eggs pass through tubes called oviducts and cells in the oviducts pour out mucus which coats the eggs on their way down. The mucus contains chemicals that absorb water and it can expand to 100 times its original size. When she squirts the eggs out from her behind, the mucus takes up water and expands into the jelly that we see.

But *why* do frogs have jelly around their eggs? Scientists disagree on the answer to this one. Maybe there's more than one answer.

Very likely the jelly keeps the eggs safe. In water, the jelly acts as a kind of padding that protects the eggs from harm.

Hey, nice pad.

Frog eggs laid on land are more likely to be knocked by something hard. They have a tough outer coat and the jelly is firmer, like the jelly you eat for dessert. These eggs keep their shape when you pick them up.

A few frog species breed in fast-flowing mountain streams where the force of the water would smash soft jelly to pulp in seconds. For eggs to survive here, the jelly has to be really tough, like a jelly snake.

The jelly has another use. It looks as though something in the jelly allows sperm to get into the eggs. Scientists have experimented by mixing eggs collected from female frogs (ones that haven't yet gone into the oviduct) with male frog sperm. Nothing happens – the sperm can't get through the membrane around the egg. But there's never any problem in fertilising eggs once they've been through the oviduct. Something in the oviducts must change the eggs as they pass through, so that sperm can get in. Experts think it might be a chemical in the jelly.

THE NOT-SO-SECRET LIFE OF TADPOLES

The fertilised egg develops into an embryo with a body and tail, and then (usually) becomes a tadpole which can swim.

Tadpoles begin life with tails but absorb them as they turn into frogs. This seems unfair, when other amphibians like salamanders and newts get to keep their tails for life.

LIFE CYCLE
OF A FROG OR TOAD

This drawing shows the most common life cycle. Some species do it differently – they have no tadpole stage. And, as you will find out, some brood their tadpoles in very odd places, like the parent's stomach or mouth!

Courting

Froglet

Mating

Tadpole or Porwiggle

Egg

Spawn

Frogs mate once a year. Some species lay only six eggs, but others can lay 30 000. Eggs and tadpoles have many enemies. Spiders, ants, fish, young dragonflies and other creatures love to eat them.

In some species, tadpoles turn into baby frogs after two weeks. Others (especially those in cold climates) remain as tadpoles for up to eighteen months.

Tadpoles start off breathing through gills, like fish, and develop lungs later. Tadpoles in hot areas grow lungs early. Warm water contains very little oxygen – above 40 degrees Celsius there is hardly any – so tadpoles in warm places like northern Australia need to be able to gulp air at the surface.

TADDIES OR TOE-BITERS

'Tadpole' is a strange word. It comes from two old English words: *Tadde* meaning toad, and *poll* meaning head. The tadpole of the toad *Bufo* has a particularly large head.

In Australia we call them 'taddies', but overseas people call them porwiggles, pollywogs, toe-biters and loggerheads!

South Pole   Icy Pole   Tadpole

CHAPTER 3

TOADILY DIFFERENT

What's the difference between a frog and a toad? Easy-peasy. Frogs are slimy but cute, toads are ugly and warty, right?

Spot the difference

Oh my God! I'm hideous!

Well, it's not quite so simple. If you said this you'd be close: 'Frogs have smooth and often slimy skins and they live in or near water. Toads have rough, dry, warty skins and they live away from water.'

But wait, there's more. There's a difference in the bones. Neither frogs nor toads have ribs, but frogs do have a sternum, a single bone down the centre of the chest. We have one too. Toads have two separate bones. Scientists gave the name *Firmisternia* to frogs (that makes sense if they have a firm sternum) and *Arcifera* to toads (*arcifera* means 'bearing a bow' and describes the bow-like shape of the halves of a toad's chest bone).

Then someone found some creatures that didn't fit the neat labels.

TOG OR FROAD?

One frog that doesn't fit the bill is the tiny *Sminthillus limbatus* of Cuba, which has half of the bone single and half double: it's arcifero-firmisternal! (Say it quickly five times.) Maybe 'tog' or 'froad' would be easier to spell.

And it turns out that so-called tree frogs have toad-like chest bones, so *they* don't fit labels either. Should they be renamed tree toads? What do you think?

Let's go back to where we started. Frogs have smooth and often slimy skins and they live in or near water. Toads have rough, dry, warty skins and they live away from water. But remember, both are tailless amphibians!

Toadily
awesome,
dude

20

TOAD TESTING

Strange but true: toads were once used for pregnancy tests in humans. Your grandparents probably learnt about your mum and dad this way (but Mum and Dad may not believe it when you tell them).

In the 1930s, two tests were used for pregnancy. One used mice, another used rabbits. In 1947 an Argentinian scientist reported that the South American toad *Bufo arenarum* would give reliable, cheap, fast results. Here's how his method worked.

A lab technician injected a small amount of a woman's urine under the skin of a male toad. After three hours, the technician collected a sample of the toad's urine, using a small glass tube, and put it under a microscope. If he or she could see many thread-like sperm moving around in it, the woman was pregnant. These were toad sperm – the urine of a pregnant woman stimulates the toad to release sperm into his cloaca, where they mix in with his urine.

Later researchers found that any frog or toad could be used (cane toads included). The test was especially useful in giving results in the first few weeks of pregnancy.

One reason why the toad test was cheap was that the same toads could be used again and again, every four days. But here comes the sad bit. The toads were not always well cared for. One report said:

> The housing of toads is easy. The only essential . . . is a high degree of moisture. The actual type of container does not matter very much as long as a rag at the bottom of it is always kept wet. The feeding problem is still simpler. The toads will not accept any kind of food one may offer them. They do quite well without any for about three or four months, and it is then time to replace them.

Why was it 'time to replace them'? Because they died – naturally, after months without food. Toads have voracious appetites, and given the chance, they'll eat every day. What they need is *living* food (live insects).

These days, laws against cruelty to animals would ensure that the toads were looked after properly.

We now have other tests to decide if a woman is pregnant.

GO TO PAGES 71-2 FOR TADPOLES AND BIRTH CONTROL

TOAD TRIP

Have you ever seen anyone drying a toad skin on their car windscreen?

It happened, in Queensland in the 1980s. People found out that dried cane-toad skin contained a powerful drug that caused hallucinations (a 'trip').

They would dry toad skins on the car windscreen, scrape them off and make a powder that could be smoked in a pipe.

This isn't new. People were using dried toad skin as snuff 3000 years ago. The chemical which causes the hallucinations, bufotenine, occurs also in the seeds of a tree in Central America, in some grasses, and in certain mushrooms which grow in many parts of the world.

Governments declared bufotenine a 'prohibited substance' and it's now illegal to own any of it.

TOAD TUNNELS

Ever heard of the road toll? – the number of deaths on our roads from car accidents? Well, we have a toad toll as well.

Two zoologists tried to work out how many amphibians and reptiles were killed each year on Australia's 103 000 km of sealed roads. They estimated the number at 5.5 million. Many of the dead are frogs and toads migrating to their breeding grounds.

In Europe, people were upset about the hundreds
of thousands of frogs that were killed on their way
to their breeding ponds. These people formed action
groups to carry frogs and toads from one side of the
road to the other. Later, toad tunnels were built
under the roads that had most frog and toad deaths.
A 'funnel fence' was added at each end to encourage
the animals into the tunnel. In 1989 the company
that builds the tunnels sponsored a Toad Tunnel
Conference in Germany.

THE CANE-TOAD CATASTROPHE

The Queensland government brought cane toads to
Australia, hoping that they would eat two kinds of beetle
that were damaging the sugar-cane crop. Sugar-cane
experts in Puerto Rico were certain they would. There
were no sprays that killed the beetles, and catching
them by hand was too hard, so bringing in cane toads
to eat them sounded like the perfect solution.

A sugar-cane specialist brought in 102 cane toads
from Hawaii, and bred from them. Thousands of baby
cane toads were then released in the cane fields of
north-eastern Australia in 1936. That was a disastrous
day for Australia.

It turned out the Puerto Rican experts were wrong.
Cane toads can't climb, so they can't reach the beetles
high up on the sugar-cane stalks. Instead they eat other
native insects and small animals. Worse, they have
caused the deaths of many birds, large lizards, snakes,
crocodiles and quolls. All these animals enjoy a frog
or toad supper. They don't know that the cane toad
is very poisonous and should be avoided, so they die.

BEST PEST TREATMENT

Plant and animal pests can often be kept
in check with chemical sprays, but it's better
if we can use other animals or insects to stop
the damage. This is called 'biological control',
and it can be better than sprays because
no poisons are involved.

Biological control worked well in an
earlier campaign against prickly pear.
This is a cactus-like plant brought in for hedges
and cattle fodder. It quickly grew out of control
and spread to cover 25 million hectares of land.
It made huge areas unfarmable. In 1913–14,
scientists released three species of moth,
three kinds of beetle and six bugs. A small
moth called *Cactoblastis* did excellent work
in chewing up zillions of prickly pear plants.
It's a pity the cane toads weren't as successful
at pest control (and were so horribly
successful as pests themselves).

Cane toads have now spread as far as Kakadu
National Park in the Northern Territory, 1800 km
from where they were first released. They are also
moving south, though not as fast, and have reached
Coffs Harbour in northern New South Wales. So far,
we haven't found any way of stopping them or saving
the native animals that they kill.

CHAPTER 4

BASKING, BURROWING, OUT AND ABOUT

FROGS TEST FOR QUALITY

Miners used to take canaries underground with them. They knew that the birds were sensitive to the poisonous gases found in mines, such as carbon monoxide. If a canary sickened, the miner knew it was time to get out.

Canaries showed if the air in a mine was healthy or not. In the same way, frogs show us when water quality is bad. Frog eggs and tadpoles live in ponds, creeks and dams, and chemicals in the water (such as insecticides sprayed onto crops to control pests) can either kill them or distort their growth. If we find lots of frogs that are missing fingers or toes, or have extra arms or legs, it could be a sign of polluted water.

(A few of these abnormalities occur naturally, but if a quarter or a third of the frogs in a pond are abnormal, then something is definitely wrong.)

WHERE DO FROGS GO IN THE DAYTIME?

A few frog species are diurnal – they are active in the daytime. Most, though, are nocturnal, active at night. Their eyes work better in low light, and they are less likely to dry out at night. So they move around, and sing to each other, at night. During the day they hide away in a cavity or burrow into the ground.

Nocturnal frogs can change their habits and behave as diurnal creatures in the breeding season, or after a shower of rain. Some will actually bask in the sun. What a life!

HOW DO FROGS FIND WATER?

We know that frogs migrate to their breeding ponds, but it is a mystery how they find their way. Do they use the stars? We don't know.

When I visited a cattle station in northern Australia, I found 24 adult Green Tree Frogs in a toilet cistern, and two more in the bowl. Not far away were at least 40 of the same frogs inside a water pump. How do 24 frogs find the same cistern? Do they tell each other? Do they smell it?

I once read a story in a magazine by a lady who lived in the Northern Territory. She had some visitors from the south who got up early and boiled the kettle for a cup of tea. They were surprised and upset when they found they'd just boiled to death an innocent frog that had been sitting inside the kettle! Unfortunately, they'd already drunk the tea.

So far no one has worked out how frogs find water.

WONDROUS WEATHER WATCHERS

Ever wanted to know if your sports match would be a washout? Simple! Consult your local frogs.

This report was written 150 years ago, by an astonished Englishman.

The green tree frogs are used in Germany as barometers; they are placed in tall bottles, with little wooden ladders. The steps of the ladder mark the air pressure; the frogs always go up towards the top in fine weather, and lower down at the approach of bad weather. I have often seen the Germans consult their frogs when starting on a 'picnic' expedition.

We have known for a long time that frogs will call in response to rain, or even when they are sprayed with a hose or sprinkler. This is called 'the rain call'. But sometimes they call *before* the rain has started. Why? I decided I had to know the answer.

You may have heard the weather person on TV talk about a 'cold front'. This is a patch of low air pressure, and often brings rain.

I wondered if frogs could sense it. To test this idea, I got a barograph (an instrument for measuring air pressure). To my surprise, the frogs started to call *before* the barograph recorded any fall in pressure preceding rain. It looks as though frogs are more sensitive to changes in air pressure than our wonderful instruments.

DESERT SURVIVORS

Frogs lose water very rapidly from their skin. Yet we can find frogs in the world's driest deserts. How do they adapt to these searing conditions?

Out in the desert sun, frogs could survive for only a few minutes. To get away from the heat, they must burrow under the surface and stay there till rain comes.

Most frogs have a pair of half-moon-shaped 'spades' near the heel. (Do you want to know the name? Outer metatarsal tubercles, or scaphoids.) Using these, they can burrow with their back feet, scraping the sand or soil outwards to the side. This leaves a dip large enough for the frog's body to slip into.

A few burrowing frogs use their hands, and have shortened, stumpy fingers and thumbs that act as spades. (They also have a thick pad of dead skin on the snout to protect it.)

As far as I know, no one has made a thorough study of frog burrows to find out how deep they go, but I've read reports of frogs being found 1.5 metres down.

water... water...

Beneath the ground, the frog lives in a small chamber or cell with hard, compacted sides. It repeatedly sheds its skin in the way frogs do, but doesn't eat it. Instead the many outgrown skins form a cocoon around its body. This cocoon reduces water loss to almost zero.

The frog is in a kind of torpor or summer sleep, called aestivation. (As you will know, animals that go into this sleep-like state in winter are in hibernation.) It can remain here without eating for up to two years.

The only way these frogs can be set free is by heavy rain – heavy enough to soften the hardened soil around them. Then they scramble to the surface, feed frantically, breed, and bury themselves again.
They may stay above ground for a month or so, eating everything they can find. As the ground dries up, the frogs burrow again.

FROGS IN THE FREEZER

If you've been to the snow, or live somewhere with very cold winters, you'll know about the anti-freeze that Dad or Mum puts in the car. The anti-freeze stops the water in your car radiator from turning into ice and splitting the radiator open.

Frogs, like reptiles, are cold-blooded, which means they can't make themselves warm. They also don't have any fur or feathers to trap heat around them.

But they have something else. Frogs that live in cold climates have an anti-freeze substance in their bodies. It's called glycerine (gliss-er-een), and it is in car anti-freeze as well.

At low temperatures, the frog goes to sleep (hibernates). Because of the glycerine it can survive temperatures of minus 10 degrees Centigrade, and maybe lower, without freezing. Pretty clever, huh?

HOW DO FROGS PROTECT THEMSELVES?

Like many other animals, frogs use colour to protect themselves. Some use colour to become near-invisible. Others use colour to scare predators away.

Many frogs can change the colour of their skin so that they blend in with the background (camouflage). For example, Roth's Tree Frog is usually dull brown, but in sunlight it turns pale cream. Some frogs (and some snakes and lizards too) have a dark stripe in front of and behind the eye, so that the eye is less obvious.

Or they may
have pointy
bits along their
arms and legs
that look like
serrated leaf edges.

Other frogs are highly coloured
– black and yellow, for instance. These
are the colours of dangerous creatures like wasps and
hornets, and 'warn' other animals to stay clear. Some
species have markings that look like eyes on their
backs, or contrasting colours on their hind legs which
are displayed when an enemy approaches.

Poison-dart frogs (see page 55–6) have
brilliant colours that make them stand out in their
environment. This tells other animals 'Watch out,
I'm poisonous. Eat me and you die.'

There is one species of frog in the Solomon Islands,
and others in South America and Asia, that will bite
any predator that comes near.

FROG NAMES
HOW TO SAY 'LONG-SNOUTED FALSE TOAD' IN LATIN

In the olden days, frogs had obvious names like bullfrog (frog with a deep call), green frog, rocket frog, fire-bellied toad, marsh toad, sandhill frog, and so on. These names are not very exact. There is probably a 'bullfrog' in every country in the world, but in fact these might be 100 different species.

What we needed was a more exact way of naming frogs (and other animals). A Swedish scientist called Carl von Linné or Linnaeus worked out a system using Latin words. People have been using the system ever since. This is how it works.

Phyllobates terribilis.

Litoria glandulosa.

The first word is a genus name (a genus is a group of closely related species). It starts with a capital: for example, *Notaden* (frog with no teeth) or *Gigantorana* (large frog – like 'gigantic').

The second word is the particular species name and doesn't have a capital. Species names sometimes refer to the person who discovered the species, or the place where it was found, or the animal's appearance or habits. *Phyllobates terribilis* sounds right for the lethal Poison-dart Frog, whose poison is indeed terrible. *Litoria cavernicola* is a good name for a frog which lives in caves and caverns in Western Australia.

The table on the next page shows some genus and species names, and what they mean. See if you can work out for yourself what a long-snouted false toad would be called. (There isn't actually a toad with this name, I made it up.)

Nigel.

SOME GENUS NAMES

Arenophryne	sand-dwelling toad
Cyclorana	round frog
Gigantorana	large frog
Glauertia	Mr Glauert
Limnodynastes	lord of the marshes
Megistolotis	big ears
Microbatrachus	small frog
Neobatrachus	new frog
Notaden	frog with no teeth
Pseudophryne	false toad

SOME SPECIES NAMES

adelaidensis	Adelaide River
albopunctatus	white-spotted
aurea	golden
bicolor	two-coloured
brevipes	short-footed
cavernicola	cave-dwelling
cryptotis	having a hidden ear
dahlii	Mr Dahl
gracilenta	slender
iris	goddess of the rainbow
longirostris	long-snouted
montana	living in mountains
nasuta	having a large nose
nigrofrenata	black-bridled
piperata	peppered
splendida	splendid, magnificent

In 1975 Marion Anstis and I found a new species of tree frog in northern New South Wales. We got out our *International Code of Zoological Nomenclature*, a big book that tells us how to give new names to animals. We named our new find *Litoria glandulosa* because it had a large gland under its chin. (Afterwards we were disappointed to find our name had already been used, for a frog found in South America in 1843. We had to find a new name and decided to call it *Litoria subglandulosa*.)

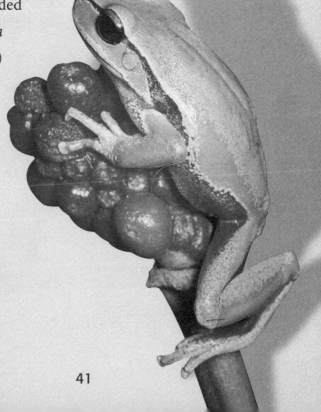

CHAPTER 5

WEIRD FROG FACTS

'RAINING CATS AND DOGS? NO, IT'S RAINING FROGS!'

There are many reports of rains of fishes, and a few of frogs. Once there were fish falling onto the roof of a house at Coffs Harbour in northern New South Wales, and fish falling at the same time on the deck of a ship off the coast.

So where do they come from?

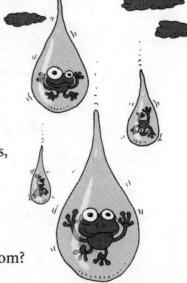

How do they get into the sky?

The most likely explanation is that they have been swept up by cyclonic winds. Cyclones can flatten buildings, lift house roofs, uproot trees. On Christmas Day 1974, Cyclone Tracy raged through Darwin, causing havoc. At one stage the cyclone picked up two cars and then dropped them into the Travelodge swimming pool. Picking up a pondful of frogs would be easy-peasy.

The whirlies or willie-willies that pluck up dust, twigs, leaves and dead bushes are smaller versions of the twisting winds at the heart of a cyclone.

FROGGY FRIDAYS IN FRANCE

Is a frog a fish? Someone once thought so – a Pope, in fact. Here's how it happened.

For centuries, Roman Catholics were not allowed to eat red meat on Friday, but they were allowed to eat fish (white meat). When the Pope said a frog was a fish, it meant that people could eat frogs on Fridays as well. So froggy Fridays were all the go.

In France, the species *Rana esculanta* (the Edible Frog) is the one most commonly eaten. In the USA, the Giant Bullfrog, *Rana catesbeiana*, is most popular because it has massive thighs.

So many frogs have been killed that France and Switzerland have started importing frogs' legs from elsewhere – thousands of tonnes of them.

French people and tourists eat up to 80 million frogs each year, and many of these used to come from India and Bangladesh. The trouble is, India and Bangladesh have almost run out of frogs.

Frog farms in Singapore, Indonesia, Malaysia and Taiwan have been very successful, and perhaps we should have many more of them.

WHAT DO FROGS' LEGS TASTE LIKE?

These days only the muscular back legs are eaten. The butcher kills the frog and chops off its back legs, then pulls off the skin like a glove. The chef will usually dust the legs with flour and fry them in butter with fresh herbs. They taste much like chicken.

Tinned or deep-frozen frogs legs' are awful, unless you like chewing wet rope.

CANNIBAL FROGS

Frogs are cannibals; they eat other frogs. I once had a particularly large female burrowing frog of the species *Cyclorana australis*. We called her Gross Gertrude. She shared a vivarium with a male not much smaller than herself, and one day expressed her love for him by swallowing him whole. She was always a ferocious feeder. If I wiggled a finger in front of her nose, she would grab and swallow as much as she could and then place her hands and feet on my palm, and try to tear the finger off!

Even in tadpoles, cannibalism is normal. Tadpoles (or porwiggles) that are injured will be eaten by their brothers and sisters. Then there are species that are 'obligate' or compulsory cannibals. They lay eggs in small patches of water that don't contain enough food for all the tadpoles that will hatch. When the food runs out, there's not much choice – they start to eat one another. The fittest (or fiercest) survive.

STICKY FEET

Have you ever seen a frog on a window? Many of them can climb perfectly smooth surfaces.

Lizards, such as geckoes, which walk up glass (or even upside-down on ceilings) have tiny curved hooks beneath their fingers and toes which latch onto microscopic cracks in a surface that to us seems quite smooth.

Frogs don't have hooks under their fingers.

Instead they have a sticky goo (mucus) on the tips of their fingers and toes which helps them climb up the glass. When they are high enough they flatten their bodies against the glass. This creates 'surface tension', a force that holds the two surfaces together. This is possible because their belly skin is loose, unlike yours and mine, which is attached to tummy muscles.

HOW SMART ARE FROGS?

Do we have a frog IQ test? No. But some people have tried to find out how good a memory frogs have.

An Englishman, Dr Cott, put toads on the ledges outside beehives. The toads ate the bees as they came in and out of the hives, and were often stung in swallowing (ouch!). After ten days, the toads realised it was the bees causing the pain. They stopped eating bees. But if they didn't see any bees for two weeks they forgot, and started snapping them up again. And so they had to re-learn the lesson.

Here's another interesting story. Mrs Lorna Brown and her husband were invited to dinner by the local health inspector in Hay, New South Wales.

When we arrived at about 7 pm, the Health Inspector said, 'You will see an amazing thing tonight – at exactly 8 o'clock a large frog will hop across the garden, come in the kitchen door, jump up on the sugar canister and wait to be fed. When we have fed him, he will hop down and go out again. He does it every day.'

I was not sure whether he was joking; however, at 8 o'clock, across the lawn hopped a large frog, into the kitchen, up on the bench and then onto the sugar canister (the centre one in a row of canisters), opened its mouth and waited to be fed. They fed it with moths and flies, and then it hopped down and went back out again.

Obviously time's fun when you're having flies!

So we know frogs and toads can learn, but may not be too good at remembering what they've learnt if the 'lesson' isn't repeated all the time.

CHAPTER 6

RECORD-BREAKERS AND CHAMPIONS

HOW OLD WAS THE OLDEST FROG?

The first question is: how do we tell how old a frog is?

Scientists can work out the age of preserved frogs in museums. They cut through the ends of the fingers and look at the edge of the bone. They see circles, like the growth rings in a tree stump. By counting the rings, they can discover how old the frog was before it died.

Here are some of the records. (These are for captive frogs. They wouldn't live as long in the wild.)

COMMON	LATIN NAME	PLACE NAME	AGE (YEARS)
Common Toad	*Bufo bufo*	UK	36
Magnificent Tree Frog	*Litoria splendida*	Australia	26
Green Tree Frog	*Litoria caerulea*	Australia	23
Cane Toad	*Bufo marinus*	Australia	23
Fire-bellied Toad	*Bombina bombina*	Eastern Europe	20
Bullfrog	*Rana catesbeiana*	USA	16
Natterjack Toad	*Bufo calamita*	Europe	16
Clawed Frog	*Xenopus laevis*	South Africa	15
Common Frog	*Rana temporaria*	UK	12
Cuban Tree Frog	*Osteopilus septentrionalis*	Cuba	12
Eastern Spadefoot Toad	*Scaphiopus holbrooki*	USA	12

Other amphibians live much longer than frogs. For example, the Giant Salamander of Japan, which grows up to 1.5 metres long, has been known to live for 55 years. (I saw the Giant Salamander at a zoo in the USA. I tried to touch its snout, and it bit me! I've also touched a galah, a possum, an emu and an owl, and have been bitten by each and every one of them. Some people never learn!)

WHAT'S THE RECORD FOR A FROG JUMP?

Every year hundreds of people go to watch (and bet on) the frog jumping competitions at the showgrounds in Angels Camp, California.[4] Each handler puts his or her frog on a green circle of felt that is supposed to represent a water-lily leaf. When the frog has done three jumps, it is captured in a net and the distance from the starting point is measured.

[4] The first published story by famous writer Mark Twain was called 'The Celebrated Jumping Frog of Calaveras County', and it described miners at Angels Camp betting on frogs.

The record at Angels Camp is 5.35 metres, but the world record is claimed to be 10.3 metres by an African species at Natal in 1977.

The secret of success is in the length of the hind legs compared to the length of the body.

WHAT IS THE BIGGEST FROG IN THE WORLD?

The winner of this contest is the Goliath Frog, *Conraua goliath*, of West Africa. The head plus body is 30 cm (the length of your ruler), and when the massive arms and long, muscly legs are stretched out, this frog measures one metre. Almost tall enough to dance with! So how heavy would this giant be? Up to 3.3 kg (about the same weight as a small dog).

Every now and then we find a single frog that is far bigger than others of the same species. This is called gigantism.

One giant Tyler's Tree Frog, *Litoria tyleri*, measured 104 mm long – normally they are under 50 mm.[5]

GO TO PAGE 82 FOR THE BIGGEST CHOCOLATE FROG

. . . AND THE SMALLEST?

We used to think that a Cuban frog, *Sminthillus limbatus*, was the smallest frog in the world. It has a head-plus-body length of up to 11.5 mm. However, a Brazilian frog, *Psyllophryne didactyla*, has now won the smallest frog title. It is no more than 9.8 mm long. Both are about the length of your thumbnail.

Baby frogs can be tiny. In some species there's no tadpole stage at all, and the frogs actually develop within the jelly. I have seen some that were only 3 mm long. (Check how long this is on your ruler.) The only way to pick up one of these froglets is to moisten the tip of your finger and touch very, very gently.

[5] This frog was named after me *(tyleri* – get it?). I am not a giant, but I am two metres tall.

So far three frogs, a mayfly, a fairy shrimp and a beetle have been named after me, but I only tell people about the frogs.

BIG MAMAS

A female frog is almost always larger than the male she chooses as a partner. (Often the largest male is larger than the smallest female, though.) This is important because of the way frogs mate. Mostly the male clasps the female by riding on her back like a jockey, so he needs to be smaller – unless the mating happens in water; then size doesn't matter much.

WHO HAS THE MOST FROGS?

So far, we've found 257 species in Sri Lanka, 250 in New Guinea, and 214 in Australia. (Australia is a frog-rich country.) Countries like Italy, Portugal, Switzerland have fewer than 20 species. At the bottom of the frog ladder are the UK and New Zealand with only four species, and Malta (a very small island) with only one. Iceland has none.

CHAPTER 7

FUNKY FROGS

POISON-DART FROGS

Indian hunters in Colombia, South America, had a great way of catching birds and animals. They used poison darts that they fired through blowpipes about two metres long. But where did they get the poison? Well, you can probably guess: from a frog. Somehow or other, the Indians had discovered that certain kinds of frog had a poison in their skin. Of the 75 known species in this group, only two gave a poison that was suitable for darts.

How did they get the poison? They held a frog over a flame to frighten it and make it secrete poison on its skin. Then they rubbed the sharp point of a dart in the poison. When they fired it at birds and small mammals in the trees through a blowpipe, the prey was instantly paralysed and fell to the ground.

How strong is the poison? The frog named *Phyllobates terribilis* contains enough poison in its skin to kill 20 000 mice! If a human being were unfortunate enough to eat a poison-dart frog they would die too.

Poison-dart frogs live in Central and South America. They are all very colourful with bright red, yellow, green or blue markings, often on a black background. These colours warn other animals to leave them alone.

Oddly enough, they make good pets. In fact, there are special clubs in countries like Holland whose members keep only poison frogs.

STOWAWAY FROGS

Seven species of Australian tree frogs live behind the 'hands' of bananas on banana palms. These spaces are dark and moist and an ideal refuge. The downside is that when the bananas are harvested, the frogs often become unwilling stowaways. They are trucked around Australia in boxes and end up at the local fruit and vegetable shop.

In Australia, a rescue scheme was introduced. Kindly truck-drivers took packages of stowaway frogs back to Queensland, so they could be released in the banana plantation that they came from. These days, they are checked for disease and given to members of the FATS (Frog and Tadpole Study) group.

The banana growers are keen to show they are good greenies, and display pictures of the Red-eyed Tree Frog in their advertisements. Unfortunately this picture shows a South American species – you can tell because the eye pupil is a vertical slit. (The Australian species has a horizontal slit.)

So, you haven't seen my banana...

Stowaway banana frogs are not unique to Australia. In the UK, frogs arrive from the Canary Islands. New Zealand receives two species of frogs in bananas from Ecuador.

FROGS THAT SUNBAKE

Frogs normally lose water through their skin very rapidly. Yet some of them bask in the sun for hours on end without drying out or being sunburnt. How do they do it?

The Australian Green Tree Frog is one of several basking species which reduce water loss by secreting wax from skin glands on the body. They then use hands and feet to wipe a thin film of this wax across their skin. The wiping is over in a few seconds, and the wax soon hardens to form an enamel-like shining coat. The basking frog remains very still, with its arms and legs tucked underneath, probably to avoid damaging the waxy film.

If we basked in the sun for several hours,

we would get badly sunburnt and blister. Frogs don't.
It seems that this wax film could also contain a special
sunscreen as well. Ver-r-ry clever!

FLYING FROGS

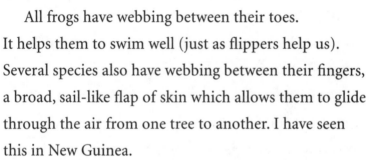

Do frogs fly? That
sounds like a silly, silly
question. But is it?

All frogs have webbing between their toes.
It helps them to swim well (just as flippers help us).
Several species also have webbing between their fingers,
a broad, sail-like flap of skin which allows them to glide
through the air from one tree to another. I have seen
this in New Guinea.

So next time you see something glide across the
air above you, you can say, 'It's a bird! It's a plane!
It's Superfrog!'

THE FROG THAT SPITS
OUT BABIES

In 1973 a new frog was discovered in South-east
Queensland, and later named the Platypus Frog.
Two young zoologists had some of these frogs in an
aquarium. One day a frog that was being handled
became distressed. It opened its mouth and spat out
tadpoles! The zoologists later sent the dead frog to
me and when I looked in its stomach I found more
tadpoles. The stomach had been expanded so much
that it was as thin as a plastic bag.

The frog now has a new name: the Southern
Gastric Brooding Frog. ('Gastric' means to do with
the stomach, like a 'gastric upset' for a tummy wog.)
Other scientists couldn't believe that a frog would
brood tadpoles in its stomach, but it's true. We now
know that the mother swallows the fertilised eggs, and
they stay in her stomach for six weeks until they turn
into tadpoles. The jelly around the eggs stops them
being digested.

Of course the mother can't eat for the six weeks.

When she opens
her mouth to let
out the baby frogs, she must be ravenous.

No one has seen any Southern Gastric Brooding
Frogs since 1981. Michael Mahony found another
stomach-brooding species in a Queensland national
park in 1984, but no one has seen any of these since
1985.

Both species are probably extinct.

FROG IN THE POND,
OR FROG IN THE POUCH?

There's a type of Australian frog called *Assa darlingtoni* – not because they are darlings, but because the person who first collected them was Dr P.J. Darlington. *Assa* is the Latin word for 'dry nurse', the nurse who cares for a child but doesn't breastfeed it.

The male frog has a pair of pouches in the skin covering his hips. As the tadpoles emerge from their jelly raft, he coats himself with the jelly, and the taddies swim into his hip pouches. They stay there until they turn into tiny froglets.

The marsupial frogs of Central and South America have a pouch on their back into which eggs are pushed. (Marsupials are animals with pouches, like kangaroos, possums, koalas.)

The strangest pouch arrangement belongs to the species *Rhinoderma darwini* of Chile.[6]

When the tadpoles hatch, the male opens his mouth to allow them to swim into it. They push through to the vocal sacs on either side of his tongue and jump in. When they have grown into baby frogs, he simply opens his mouth, and out they hop!

Like the gastric brooding frogs, the male *Rhinoderma* has to stop eating – and croaking – for several weeks.

[6] The word *dermus* means skin, but *Rhinoderma* doesn't mean skin like a rhinoceros! *Rhino* means something to do with the nose, and these frogs have big noses that stick out a lot. *Darwini* comes from Charles Darwin, 'the father of evolution', a great and famous scientist long ago.

FROG NUMBERS
GOING UP OR COMING DOWN?

People keep on finding more frog species. In 1975, experts said there 2500 species around the world. Ten years later, 59 amphibians experts drew up a new list, with 4003 names on it. Today the total is at least 5000.

Why did it take so long to discover the new species? For some reason I cannot understand, early explorers concentrated on warm and cuddly creatures such as koalas, or brilliantly coloured birds and butterflies. Frogs just weren't appreciated.

It's also true that some frogs are difficult to find. We may well discover more species in hard-to-get-to parts of the world, especially in the tropics where frogs are abundant. I think we'll end up with close to 6000 frog and toad species.

How does this compare with other animals? So far we know of 22 000 fish, 5000 mammals, 6500 reptiles and 10 000 birds. There are so many kinds of insects that I don't want to be the one to count them.

WHY ARE SOME FROGS DYING OUT?

We're finding new species, but some of the old ones are in trouble. Some years ago I was invited to join a frog taskforce. We found that some frogs were doing well, but many were endangered, and some had become extinct. We tried to work out why. Here's what we found.

Global warming hasn't been severe enough (yet) to explain the problems.

Increased ultra-violet (UV) radiation might be a cause, but we're not sure.

Chemical pollution is bad news for frogs.

• Weed- and bug-killers sprayed by farmers or by council workers can get into creeks and ponds and cause abnormal bone growth.

• The surfactants in weed-killers, and in soap and shampoo, are deadly to frogs and fish (see pages 66–7).

• Some chemicals interfere with breeding.

Recently we've found a soil fungus that suffocates frogs (we think) by attacking their skin. (Remember, they breathe through their skin.)

There's no one thing that is causing all our frogs' problems. But it is clear that we need a cure for the fungus and much less pollution of all kinds for frogs to survive.

SAVING FROG LIVES

There are two useful things humans could do to stop frog deaths. One is to avoid using herbicides with surfactants near creeks and ponds, or near the hollows where puddles form. These are the places used for frog spawning. Wetting agents used in the soil by home gardeners are just as bad.

The other thing is to not use shampoo near water when we're camping. Shampoo also has surfactants in it. The Northern Territory has a rule that campers must not use shampoo within 50 metres of water.

WHY SURFACTANTS ARE DEADLY

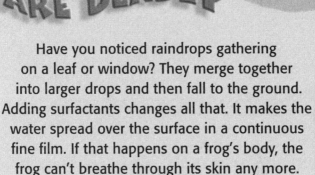

Have you noticed raindrops gathering on a leaf or window? They merge together into larger drops and then fall to the ground. Adding surfactants changes all that. It makes the water spread over the surface in a continuous fine film. If that happens on a frog's body, the frog can't breathe through its skin any more.

A simple experiment shows how surfactants work. Take a clean plastic container (the kind used for margarine or butter is fine). Fill it with water and sprinkle finely ground pepper on the surface. Then take a tiny piece of soap (which is a surfactant) and touch the surface of the water with it. The pepper races to the edge of the container. The soapy layer covers the entire surface.

CHAPTER 8

FROG FOLKLORE

'NEVER TOUCH A TOAD, YOU'LL GET WARTS'

This is an ancient belief and a false one. Toads do have lumps on their skin, but they are not warts. Warts are caused by viruses. Toad lumps are natural.

The truth may be the other way round. There's an equally ancient recipe for getting rid of warts: rub the wart with a dry, dusty toad. Don't laugh, this could be close to the truth.

Recently, research scientists showed that frog glands produce chemicals which can help get rid of *Herpes simplex*, a virus that causes blisters. The Australian Tree

Frog, *Litoria caerulea*, secretes a substance called caerin which protects it against other viruses.

CURES FOR WARTS

1 Rub the wart with rancid bacon rind, then bury the rind. When it decays, the wart will disappear.

2 Cut a potato, rub it on the wart, then throw it over the fence.

3 Rub the gizzard of a chicken on the wart during the waning of the moon. Bury the gizzard in the middle of a dirt road.

4 Apply the milk from a thistle twice daily. Within three weeks, the wart will vanish.

5 Sell your wart to a friend or relative and soon it will disappear, as it no longer belongs to you.

Have you ever had warts? How did you make them go away?

IS THE BOILING FROG THEORY TRUE?

Someone once suggested that if a frog is dropped in a pot of boiling water it will jump out straight away, but if it is put in cool water that is slowly brought to the boil it won't notice and will die. In the same way, perhaps people don't notice gradual change is making things worse until it's too late.

As far as frogs are concerned, I can say that frogs are highly sensitive to temperature change. Their lives depend on that ability. The Boiling Frog Theory is definitely wrong.

Do frogs feel pain? I'm certain they do.

Humans have a built-in alarm system. When our bodies are being damaged (or are about to be damaged), we feel pain. Then we shout for help, or snatch our hand away from the fire, or do whatever we need to do to prevent harm.

Frogs have a nervous system much like ours, so they must feel pain. The question is: can they show it? How can we tell when it's happening?

We have face muscles that show other people what we're feeling – shock, concern, horror, anger, pleasure, pain. Frogs have few face muscles, and none that could show feelings, at least to us. All they can do is hop away.

FROGS AND FERTILITY

Fifty years ago, a government official in China said that women could stop having so many babies by eating tadpoles. (The Chinese government was very worried about having too many people and not enough food for them.)

Fresh tadpoles should be washed clean then swallowed alive three or four days after menstruation. If a woman swallows fourteen live tadpoles on the first day and ten more the following day, she will not conceive [get pregnant] for five years.

He said that if the woman repeated the steps, she would be sterile for life – she'd never, ever have any children.

What happened? Soon there were hardly any tadpoles left in nearby creeks, but women continued to have babies.[7]

The Inca people of South America had the reverse idea. They thought frogs would help them to have *more* babies, and wore frog brooches and necklaces to help make it happen. Pictures of frogs on the walls of Egyptian tombs may have the same purpose. It makes sense when you know that some species of frogs lay tens of thousands of fertilised eggs at a time.

GO TO PAGES 21–2 TO FIND OUT ABOUT TOADS AND PREGNANCY TESTING

---

[7] A Chinese taxi driver thought, 'Aha! I can go one better.' He wanted a contraceptive for himself. He decided to swallow live frogs rather than tadpoles, but choked on the third one and died.

FROGGY MEDICINES

Dried frogs are used in Chinese medicine. (So are crocodile gall bladders, deer sinews, rhino horn and other surprising animal parts.) I have seen the dried frogs, just skeletons with a few muscles holding them together. The instructions are to break off the head and throw it away, then steam or boil the rest for 1–3 hours. Throw out the frog remains and drink the fluid as a tonic. Hmmm.

Much more likely to be useful are creams for ulcers and skin infections. Many frog species have glands in their skin that produce antibiotic compounds and anti-inflammatory steroids. Ointments using these substances could be very helpful to humans.[8]

FROG GODS

Long ago in the city of Babylon there was a story about the origin of the Earth. The story described land emerging from beneath the ocean. On the land were eight gods and goddesses, and four of the gods were frogs! In ancient Egypt the Goddess Heket's symbol was a frog.

[8] Violinists used to hold toads in their hands before playing. They believed that secretions in the toad skin would stop them getting too sweaty.

DREAMTIME FROGS

Aborigines hardly ever eat frogs, preferring kangaroo, wallaby, goanna and large birds. But frogs have been very important to Aborigines in desert areas, because they supply water. The Aborigines squeezed the frogs to make them release fluid from their bladders. Frog urine is very dilute, much like pure water.

Frogs also figure in some Dreamtime stories. The best-known myth is about Tiddalik, the frog who drank up all the water on Earth, and later was made to laugh to let the water out again.

This story fits well with the sudden floods that occasionally happen in outback Australia.

CHAPTER 9

'DOWN, FREDDO!'

Probably the most popular frog pet is the Australian Green Tree Frog (also known as 'White's Tree Frog'). These frogs are sold at pet shops in many countries, and are bred in large numbers for this purpose.

They will sit on the keeper's hand and not try to jump away. They are easy to feed and don't seem to mind being kept in captivity.

They will live for up to 23 years, and people become very fond of them. The longer they live, the more you love them.

I have friends who keep two frogs, one of which is greedy. To make sure that the smaller one doesn't miss out on its share of the food (live crickets), my friends feed the frogs on the coffee table, one at a time.

HOW TO MAKE A FROGGY PARADISE FOR YOUR PET

Probably the best home for a frog is a glass aquarium. You can make a good frog habitat by putting a small bowl of water, and another bowl for food, into a layer of peat at the bottom of the aquarium. (You can buy peat from a gardening shop.) Tree frogs will climb up the glass walls, but it is a good idea to put a dead branch inside because they like to get off the ground to rest.

Some people place small pebbles in the aquarium. This is dangerous because the frogs may accidentally swallow them along with the insect they leap at. Bigger pebbles or stones are all right – just make sure they are much larger than the frog's mouth.

You need a good lid for your frog home. Don't use glass – it doesn't let in any air. I use a wooden frame

covered with flywire. You can tape it to the glass.
It needs to be a snug fit, otherwise the frogs will push
it up at night and escape. You'll be playing 'hide
and seek' for a very long time (check under the fridge
and washing machine).

FEEDING

Frogs don't chew their
food; they swallow
it whole. Most catch
their prey with their
sticky tongue, but a few
(with absolutely no table
manners) stuff it in
with their hands.

Live insects are by far the
commonest food. Frog-keepers feed their frogs with
'mealworms' or with crickets. These can be bought
at pet shops. Beetles, cockroaches and moths are
also acceptable. You can catch moths in the evening
when they are attracted to lights around your home.

It is fascinating
to watch a frog
leap inside its
aquarium and catch a
flying moth in mid-air,
but it's so quick you'll want
a replay.

Frogs will only eat living
food – it has to be moving to be
recognised as food. Some pets will
eat a dead insect if you hold the food
lightly in a pair of tweezers (plastic like
the ones in first-aid kits), and wave it in
front of them. If you wave it well, they'll
think it's alive.

WEIGHT WATCH

If we lived in a small room, had no exercise and ate
as much and as often as we liked, we would almost
certainly become overweight. Pet frogs often have the
same problem.

Frogs don't put on fat all over their body and limbs as we do. Instead, they store the fat in 'fat bodies' along the spine, inside the body cavity. If a pet frog is fed more than it needs, the fat bodies become huge and literally fill all available space. I'm not sure if this would kill the frog, but it's certainly not healthy.

One or two meals a week is quite enough for a frog that doesn't get any exercise. If it eats everything offered to it day after day, perhaps it's bored rather than hungry.

If you can, let your frog exercise. This is hard to do for a small, skittish frog, but tame frogs that are happy to be handled can be allowed to roam outside the cage – just keep a careful eye (or two) on them.

CHAPTER 10

THE POPULARITY OF FROGS

Everyone is fascinated by frogs. Almost every child collects frog spawn and watches the change from tadpole to frog. I did, and I'm sure you have too!

They appear in jewellery, garden statues and toys.

We love them so much that we have chocolate frogs, frog wine and frog cakes. They show up on posters, postcards, letterheads, postage stamps, eyedrops and cough medicine ('I've got a frog in my throat').

If you keep your eyes open, you'll find frogs being used in advertising. Whenever a company wants to show that it cares about the environment, it will use a frog for its logo: a green frog for a green environment.

The table opposite shows just how popular frogs are.

THE **MOST** POPULAR FROGS OF ALL: CHOCOLATE FROGS

Chocolate frogs have been around for almost 100 years. Cadbury's 'Freddo Frogs' are perhaps the most famous. Pink Lady Chocolates tried something different. They added a green foil wrapper showing an endangered species, the Green and Golden Bell Frog of New South Wales. By far the biggest frog on the market is the Super Frog produced by Haigh's Chocolates, which weighs in at 265 grams and is about one centimetre thick. You almost need a saw to cut it!

	SLUGS	EARWIGS	SLATERS	FROGS
Cakes	-	-	-	√
Chocolates	-	-	-	√
Doorstops	-	-	-	√
Soap bars	-	-	-	√
Ornaments	-	-	-	√
Bookmarks	-	-	-	√
Paperweights	-	-	-	√
Toys	-	-	-	√
Cartoons	-	-	-	√
Postage stamps	-	-	-	√
Wine labels	-	-	-	√
Carvings	-	-	-	√
Key rings	-	-	-	√
Brooches	-	-	-	√
String dispensers	-	-	-	√
Watering cans	-	-	-	√
Garden ornaments	-	-	-	√
TV films	-	-	-	√
Tablecloth weights	-	-	-	√
Ties	-	-	-	√

MIKE TYLER has been mad about frogs since he was a boy, which is quite a while ago. He is known around the world as 'The Frogman' and has found out enough about frogs and toads to write 24 books. Even so, he has admitted that he can't stomach frogs' legs, which he says taste like wet rope. (Correction: *tinned* frogs' legs taste like wet rope.)

Michael Tyler is an Associate Professor at the University of Adelaide.

MIC LOOBY is an illustrator and writer who lists his hobbies as chewing pens and humming softly.

THANKS

I am grateful to Bill Branch, Vivienne Mitchell, Alan Channing, Kerry Dohring, John Dowie, Emily Downes, Eric Mathews, Chuck Myers, Brian Pridmore and Paul E. Tyler for proposing questions or providing information about some of the topics.

The contribution of Sarah Brenan, the series editor at Allen & Unwin, has been fantastic. Sarah has guided me through the process of converting my original words to a book that we hope will be appealing to readers. I thank her for being patient and extremely supportive.

Finally I wish to acknowledge the most constructive help that I have received from Bronwynne Green during the preparation of the manuscript. She picked up the flaws that I had missed, made numerous useful suggestions and encouraged me throughout the writing and design of the book. I am deeply indebted to her.

Mike Tyler

The publishers would like to thank the following for photographs used in the text: Densey Clyne for those on pages i, 8, 28, 37, 41, and Michael Tyler for those on pages viii, 61.

GLOSSARY

aestivation semi-sleeping state in summer

bufotenine a chemical contained in cane-toad skin and in certain plants and mushrooms that gives you hallucinations when you eat it

cloaca the hole in a frog's bottom used for getting rid of waste and for mating

contraceptive anything that prevents sperm fertilising eggs, and so stops babies being made

ecdysis the process of sloughing or shedding old skin

embryo a young animal in the earliest stages of development

fertilise make ready to reproduce

genus a group of closely related species

hibernation sleeping state of some animals in winter

keratin a hard, tough substance that makes up tadpole teeth and animal hair, feathers, horns and hoofs

membrane a thin layer of cells or 'skin' between two substances

mucus sticky stuff, like snot and spit

oviducts tubes or passages inside a female frog which eggs pass through

secrete to ooze or produce

slough to throw off or shed or separate from (skin)

spawn a mass of fertilised eggs in the water. Each egg is surrounded by jelly.

species a group of similar individuals that can breed together

sperm a male cell that joins a female cell to start a new baby frog (or other animal or person)

vivarium a container or home for live animals that provides an environment similar to their natural habitat (an aquarium is a watery vivarium)

WHERE TO FIND OUT MORE

Books

Kevin Casey, *Attracting Frogs to Your Garden*, Kimberley Publications, Brisbane, 1996

Michael Tyler, *Australian Frogs. A Natural History*, Reed/New Holland, Sydney, 2000

Michael Tyler, *Frogs as Pets*, Graphic Print Group, Richmond, South Australia, 1996

Videos

Frogs – The Tyler Tapes, Freshwater Films, PO Box 86, Point Lookout, Qld 4183

Websites

- http://www.exploratorium.edu/frogs/mainstory/index.html
- http://latham.dropbear.id.au/frogs/
- http://www.asxfrogfocus.com/
- http://www.allaboutfrogs.org/froglnd.shtml
- http://www.frogs.org.au

  Click 'Launchpad' for organisations in states other than Victoria.

For teachers

An Atlas of Queensland's Frogs, Reptiles, Birds and Mammals, ed. Glen J. Ingram and Robert J. Raven, Queensland Museum, Brisbane, 1991

Marion Anstis, *Tadpoles of South-eastern Australia*, Reed/New Holland, Sydney, 2002

John Barker, Gordon Grigg and Michael Tyler, *A Field Guide to Australian Frogs*, Surrey Beatty and Sons, Chipping Norton, New South Wales, 1995

Jean-Marc Hero, Murray Littlejohn and Gerry Marantelli, *Frogwatch Field Guide to Victorian Frogs*, Department of Conservation and Environment, Victoria, 1991

Michael Tyler and Margaret Davies, *Frogs of the Northern Territory*, Conservation Commission of the Northern Territory, Darwin, 1986

Michael Tyler, L. A. Smith and R. E. Johnston, *Frogs of Western Australia*, 3rd edition, Western Australian Museum, Perth, 2000

INDEX